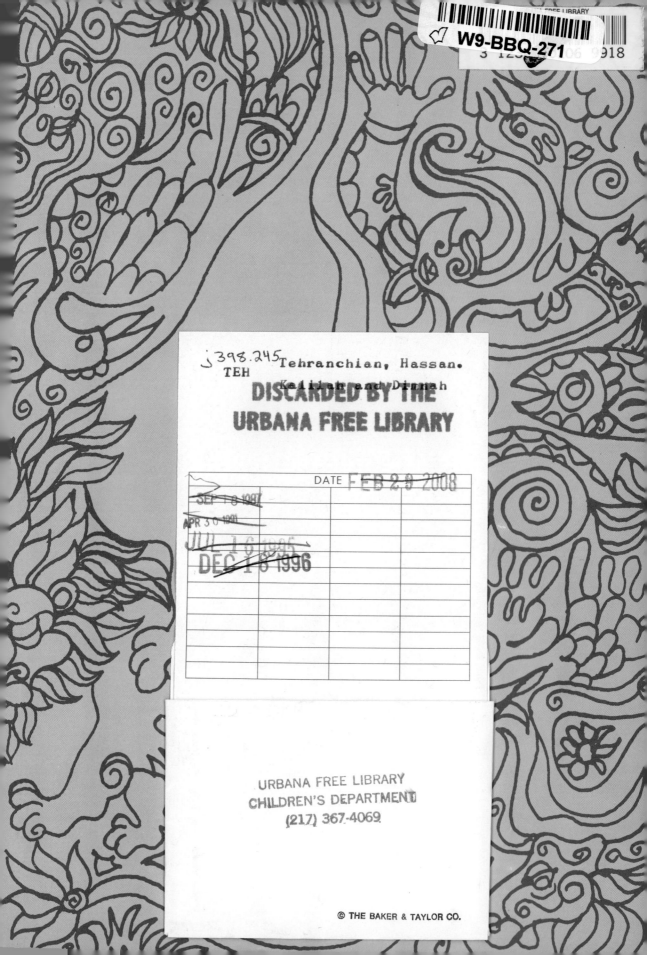

Kalilah and Dimnah

FABLES FROM
THE ANCIENT EAST

KALILAH AND DIMNAH

Translated from the Persian and adapted by
Hassan Tehranchian

Illustrations by Anatole Ur

Harmony Books/New York

COPYRIGHT © 1985 BY HASSAN TEHRANCHIAN AND ANATOLE UR

All rights reserved. No part of this book may be reproduced or transmitted
in any form or by any means, electronic or mechanical, including
photocopying, recording, or by any information storage and retrieval
system, without permission in writing from the publisher.

Published by Harmony Books, a division of Crown Publishers, Inc.,
One Park Avenue, New York, New York 10016
and simultaneously in Canada by General Publishing Company Limited

HARMONY and colophon are trademarks of Crown Publishers, Inc.

Manufactured in Hong Kong

Library of Congress Cataloging in Publication Data
Tehranchian, Hassan.
Kalilah and Dimnah: from the ancient East.
1. Fables, Persian—Translations into English.
2. Fables, English—Translations from Persian.
I. Kalilah wa-Dimnah. II. Title.
PR9507.9.T4K3 1985 398.2′45′0955 84-25289
ISBN: 0-517-55566-2

Designed by Claudia Carlson

10 9 8 7 6 5 4 3 2 1

First Edition

CONTENTS

INTRODUCTION

Kalilah and Dimnah, an ancient series of fables from the East, has delighted and amused adults and children for centuries. The origin of the tales, which take their names from two jackals appearing in the first two chapters of the text, was a matter of controversy for some time. However, when two Sanskrit texts, *Panchatantra and Mahabharata*, became available to the scholars for the first time, there remained no doubt that the book originated in India.

Panchatantra is a collection of Indian fables gathered by an unknown Brahman during the third century A.D. In its original form, *Panchatantra* had been a treatise on state-craft intended to train Indian princes for their kingly profession. The text contains five chapters, all of which are found in *Kalilah and Dimnah*.

Mahabharata, a great epic, according to some scholars, surpassing even the *Iliad* of Homer, was compiled even earlier by many unknown contributors. Three chapters of *Kalilah and Dimnah* are adapted from the *Mahabharata*. Except for the segments added to the text by different translators, the rest of *Kalilah and Dimnah* also has an Indian origin.

Kalilah and Dimnah was first translated from the Sanskrit into the old Persian tongue of Pahlavi under the reign of the Sasanian king, Khusrau Anushirvan (A.D. 531–579) by Burzuyeh, the king's physician, who traveled to India in search of a medicinal plant and returned instead with a manuscript. The manuscript, afterward called *Kalilah and Dimnah*, was compiled by Burzuyeh, who collected a series of fables from different Indian sources and added new tales to them himself. By King Anushirvan's behest, a new chapter was also added to honor Burzuyeh.

Two centuries later in A.D. 750, the Arab scholar Abd Allah ibn al-Moqafa translated *Kalilah and Dimnah* from Persian into Arabic. Since no copy of the Pahlavi version of the text has reached us, it is difficult to clarify the changes that ibn al-Moqafa made.

Afterward, several Iranian scholars and poets translated ibn al-Moqafa's version of *Kalilah and Dimnah* from Arabic back into Persian. The translation done by Nasr Allah Munshi in 1156 came to be the most popular. The beauty of Nasr Allah's writing has made his translation a treasure of Persian literature, lending depth to the interaction of the different animals and giving credibility to their universe.

The view of animals found in *Kalilah and Dimnah* derives from the Indian belief that animals have personality, awareness, and live in a world much like that of human beings. In the world of *Kalilah and Dimnah,* animals as well as human beings are found to be at the mercy of their own and each other's passions. Dimnah's story, as we will observe in the present book, is a result of his own jealousy and ambition. For this reason, his character reminds us of Shakespeare's Iago and Richard III. The jackal as human being and the human being as the jackal!

It is this transformation, the animal appearing as human being and the human mind appearing in the animal body, that fascinates both children and adults. In the wondrous realm of the animal kingdom we discover our own moral issues. Here is the clear world of virtue and morality, alongside the dark world of malevolence and immorality. We witness the clash of these two worlds, an everlasting conflict between good and evil. Is not this conflict, indeed, a reflection of our own daily life?

The present book, translated from Persian and adapted for children, consists only of two chapters of *Kalilah and Dimnah.* The Persian text used for the translation is Nasr Allah Munshi's version which has been collated by the late scholar Mujtaba Minuvi and published by the University of Tehran in 1965. The division of this book into five chapters is done for the purpose of simplification and is not, in any way, related to the original Persian text.

I hope that my effort in preserving the main concepts of the text in translation and adaptation has been successful. If so, then the English-speaking children of the world will find it not only entertaining but also enlightening.

I
A KING'S ADVISER

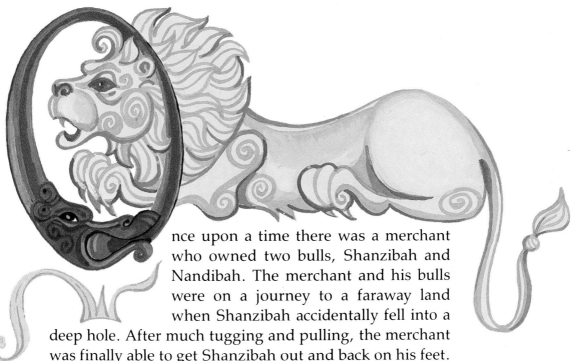

nce upon a time there was a merchant who owned two bulls, Shanzibah and Nandibah. The merchant and his bulls were on a journey to a faraway land when Shanzibah accidentally fell into a deep hole. After much tugging and pulling, the merchant was finally able to get Shanzibah out and back on his feet. But the poor animal was so injured that he could not travel any farther. So the merchant found a man to take care of Shanzibah until he was better.

The man was supposed to return Shanzibah to the merchant when the bull had recovered. But, after only one day, the untrustworthy man became tired and bored.

He left the poor, unhappy animal all alone and returned to the merchant, telling him that Shanzibah had died.

But fortune smiled on Shanzibah and he recovered all by himself, and set out to find food. To his amazement, he came upon a beautiful field that was full of brightly colored flowers and vegetables of all kinds. Shanzibah rested, and ate so well that he soon became healthy again. He felt so lucky and happy that one day, out of pure joy, Shanzibah let out a very loud bellow.

At the same time there was a lion who lived near the field. This lion was the king of many other animals. Although he was strong and brave, he had never seen a bull or heard one bellow before, so when he heard Shanzibah's loud voice he became very frightened. But since the lion did not want the other animals to know that he was afraid, he decided to stay close to home, instead of roaming far and wide all over his kingdom, as he used to.

Among the lion's subjects were two clever jackals named Kalilah and Dimnah. One day Dimnah, who was more ambitious and greedy, asked Kalilah, "Why do you think the lion has been staying at home so much lately?"

Puzzled by the question, Kalilah answered, "Why are you so interested in the king? It's really none of our business. We are comfortable and rich under the lion's rule, and besides, we're not friendly enough with the king to give him advice. It would be better to mind your own

business and leave the king's alone, because if you try to do something you don't know how to do, you might end up like the monkey.''

"What do you mean?'' asked Dimnah.

The Monkey and The Carpenter

Kalilah explained: Once a monkey saw a carpenter sawing a piece of wood. The carpenter used two nails to keep the wood balanced. He would pound one nail into the wood and then pull the other nail out. For some reason, the carpenter had to leave his work in the middle, and the monkey was left alone. He sat on the piece of wood and decided to do the carpenter's job. After all, it looked easy. But, before pounding one nail into the wood, he pulled the other nail out. Suddenly the wood broke into two pieces and sprang together with great force, catching the monkey's tail between them. His tail was squeezed so hard that he fainted, and when the carpenter came back he was so angry that he beat the monkey to death. This is where the saying "Carpentry is not a monkey's job'' comes from.

After listening to the story, Dimnah said, "I understand the point of your story, but that has nothing to do with

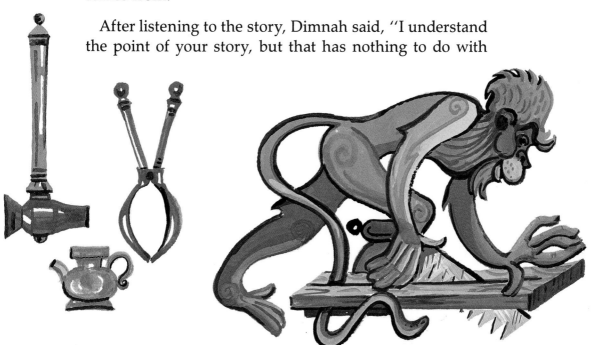

Not every powerful voice comes from a strong body.

becoming an adviser to the king. An adviser would become a very important person."

"That is true," remarked Kalilah, "but you've got to understand that we are only jackals and would not be considered for such high positions."

Dimnah answered cleverly, "Only ambitious and hard-working people reach high positions. If someone works very hard he can raise his position in life. On the other hand, a weak person will cause his own downfall. We should seek higher positions and not be satisfied with what we have now."

"Then," demanded Kalilah, "tell me what you have in mind."

Dimnah explained: "I would like to introduce myself to the lion. He is upset, and I'm sure I can make him happy with my advice. By doing that I will win his confidence."

"But," asked Kalilah, "how do you know that the lion is upset?"

"I know it because I am so intelligent," said Dimnah. "An intelligent man can sense when something is wrong."

"But," answered Kalilah, "how are you going to become an adviser to the lion? You have never served a king before."

Dimnah had a ready answer. "The king's attendants

were not given their ranks and positions all at once; they slowly were moved up from lower positions. If I can get close to the lion I will try to understand him and I will be honest and obedient. I will encourage him to act in a way that will help his people. And when I disagree with his plans, I will try, without offending him, to show what will happen if he follows his own plan. I will be so honest and helpful that I will become his most important adviser. When the lion recognizes my knowledge and skill he will appreciate me much more.''

But Kalilah was still uneasy. "If you have really decided to do this," he advised Dimnah, "you must be aware that what you want to do is very dangerous. According to wise men, only foolish men do these three things: become involved in the king's business; taste poison in order to see what it is; and tell secrets to women!"

Dimnah answered, "That is all true. But the one who never takes chances never becomes great. Let me remind you that only a strong and courageous man could do these three things: enter into the king's business; do business by sea; and face one's enemy."

So Dimnah went to court and introduced himself to the lion. The lion asked his attendants if they knew who Dimnah was, and they told him all they knew about Dimnah and his family. The lion remembered Dimnah's father and so was friendly. He asked Dimnah where he lived. Dimnah replied, "I am staying at my lord's court, waiting for a position so that I can prove myself to you. For any servant, no matter how poor he is, can be of some use one day."

The lion was pleased with Dimnah's response and told his attendants that "a wise man, even if he is of low rank, stands out in a crowd because of his honesty and wisdom."

When he heard this remark, Dimnah became very happy. He realized that he had already impressed the lion. So he dared to suggest, "Let all the subjects present their advice to my lord and show their knowledge openly. If my lord does not know how much knowledge his subjects have, he cannot really benefit from their service. Knowledge is like a seed that is ignored as long as it is hidden beneath the earth. After it grows, people can enjoy taking care of it and gain profit from it. It is important that my lord give his subjects positions based on knowledge and ability, not only on family lineage. He should not prefer careless, unskilled people over learned and wise men. Surrounding himself with friends who have no skills is dangerous. Great things are accomplished by knowledgeable and experienced men; not only by friends or those who stay close to you. Remember, a man who carries a small ruby does not become tired, and the ruby can be very valuable in a time of need. On the other hand, a man who carries a bag of heavy rocks soon becomes tired, and

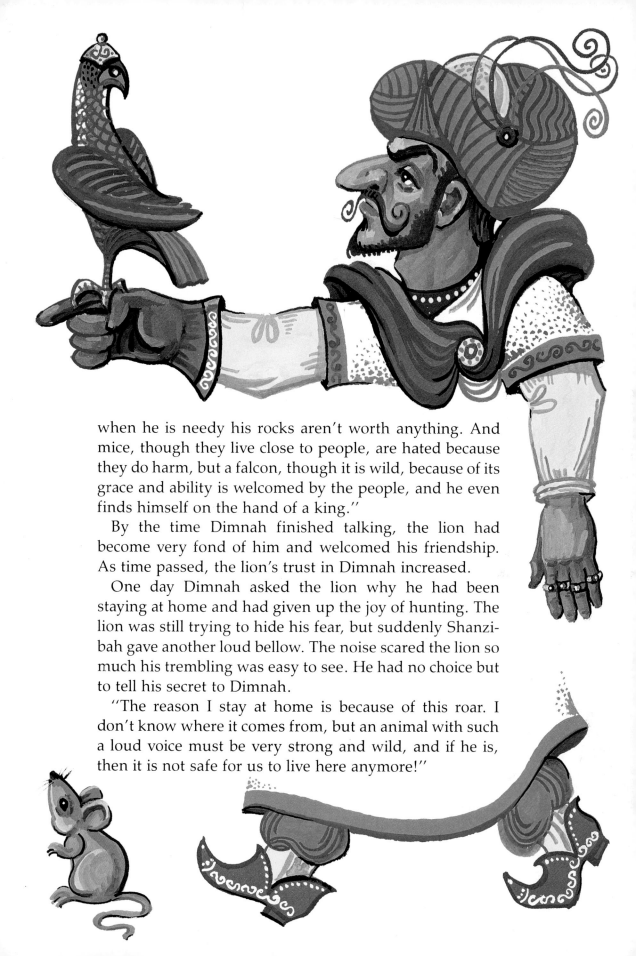

when he is needy his rocks aren't worth anything. And mice, though they live close to people, are hated because they do harm, but a falcon, though it is wild, because of its grace and ability is welcomed by the people, and he even finds himself on the hand of a king.''

By the time Dimnah finished talking, the lion had become very fond of him and welcomed his friendship. As time passed, the lion's trust in Dimnah increased.

One day Dimnah asked the lion why he had been staying at home and had given up the joy of hunting. The lion was still trying to hide his fear, but suddenly Shanzibah gave another loud bellow. The noise scared the lion so much his trembling was easy to see. He had no choice but to tell his secret to Dimnah.

''The reason I stay at home is because of this roar. I don't know where it comes from, but an animal with such a loud voice must be very strong and wild, and if he is, then it is not safe for us to live here anymore!''

Dimnah asked if there was anything else besides the roar that frightened the lion, and the lion said, "No."

Then Dimnah said, "It doesn't seem right for my lord to leave his own land because of a loud roar. Besides, not every powerful voice or large body means something is strong. "What do you mean?" asked the lion. Dimnah explained.

The Fox and The Drum

Once a fox crossing a field saw a drum fall near a tree. The wind caused a branch of the tree to pound on the drum, making a loud noise. The fox, who was impressed by the size of the drum and the loud sound it made, thought it would surely have lots of juicy meat. So the fox tried to tear the drum apart, but he only found a little thin skin. Then the fox told himself, 'I should have known that the larger the body and the louder the voice, the less substance it would have.'

"I told this story," said Dimnah, "so that my lord would see that he has no reason to be afraid. And, if my lord wishes, I will go to investigate the habits of this wild thing." The lion thought this was a good idea indeed.

When Dimnah came back, the lion rushed to ask him what he had found out. Dimnah reported, "I saw an ordinary bull, without the proud looks that go with great strength."

But this did not comfort the lion. He replied, "What you saw does not prove the bull is weak, either. As you know, a strong wind that can knock down huge trees may not be able to uproot a small bush."

Dimnah assured the lion that he must not worry. "If my lord agrees, I will bring the bull back here to be an obedient subject." The lion happily agreed.

So Dimnah went to Shanzibah and said, "I have been sent by the lion, who has ordered me to take you to him. If you come with me, I will ask him to forgive you for not introducing yourself to him sooner. But if you refuse, I will return at once and report your disobedience."

"Who is this lion?" asked Shanzibah.

"The king of all the wilds," answered Dimnah.

The title "king of all the wilds" terrified Shanzibah. He asked Dimnah whether he would protect him if he went with him. Dimnah promised him he would be safe, so Shanzibah went along.

The lion welcomed Shanzibah warmly. He asked him when and why he had come to the kingdom. Shanzibah told his story to the lion, who liked Shanzibah so much he invited him to stay in the field as his guest. Shanzibah was so thankful he offered his services in return. After testing Shanzibah's knowledge in various ways, the lion decided he could trust him and made him a close friend. Day by day, Shanzibah's rank and position became higher and higher, until he became the lion's most trusted adviser.

A ruler should never
ignore his advisers.

II
THE DECEIVER'S PLOT

But after a while, Dimnah became very jealous because of the lion's kindness toward Shanzibah. He went to Kalilah and complained bitterly. "Oh, brother! Do you see how stupid I was? I tried so hard to free the lion from his fear that I didn't pay enough attention to my own future. I introduced Shanzibah to the lion, and now *he* has been promoted to a high position, while I have lost my importance."

Kalilah felt sorry for his friend and asked, "What are you going to do now?"

Dimnah said: "I am trying to think of a way to reverse Shanzibah's wheel of fortune; and, since I am not seeking a higher position at this time, no one will be able to accuse me of ambition. There are three things that wise men try to do: earn the good things that should have been earned in the past; obtain the good things in the present; and secure good things for the future. And because I am full of hope, I will surely accomplish my goal.

"The best way," continued Dimnah, "is to make up a plan to have Shanzibah killed. I believe that since the lion has left everything to Shanzibah, he himself has become weak. So it is really in his own best interest that Shanzibah be killed."

Kalilah did not think things were so simple, but he said: "I agree with you that the lion has been too generous in raising Shanzibah's position."

Dimnah added: "And the king has ignored and upset his other advisers too, so he has lost their friendship. There are six things that are enemies of the state: deprivation, rebellion, desire, bad luck, bad temper, and stupidity. Deprivation is when the ruler deprives himself of the company of wise men. Rebellion is when unexpected wars break out. Desire is devotion to wine, women, and pleasures of the senses. Bad luck is when cholera, famine, flood, fire occur. Bad temper is when the king rules badly in anger. And stupidity is when the king is kind to those who are hostile and hostile to those who are friends."

"I understand these points," Kalilah answered, "but how are you going to kill Shanzibah? He is much stronger than you and has surrounded himself with many people."

"That doesn't matter," answered Dimnah. "Things can be brought about by knowledge and cleverness that can't be done by strength and force. Haven't you heard the story about the raven who killed a snake?"

"No," answered Kalilah.

The Raven and The Snake

Dimnah said: There once was a raven who made her house in a tree on a high mountain. In her neighborhood lived a wicked snake who liked to eat the raven's children. At last the raven couldn't stand it anymore. She discussed the problem with a jackal who happened to be her friend. "I will try to blind the snake while he's asleep, in order to protect my children."

"But this is not a wise thing to do," warned the jackal. "A smart person doesn't risk his own life to fight an enemy. Don't act like the heron who tried to kill the crab but put his own life in danger."

"Tell me the story," the raven asked. The jackal did.

The Heron and The Fish

Once there was a heron with a long skinny neck, long skinny legs, and a long skinny beak, who lived near a pond. Each day he caught as many fish as he needed, and he lived a very comfortable life. However, when he grew old he was not able to catch fish as easily as when he was young. The heron regretted not having saved anything for his old age. But because he was so clever, he came up with an idea to catch the food he needed every day.

The heron sat beside the pool one day and pretended to be very sad. A large red crab who lived in the pond saw him from far away. He came to the heron and said, "You seem to be very unhappy."

"How can I be happy?" answered the heron sadly. "My daily meal comes from this pond. Usually I catch one or two fish each day, and nobody notices their loss. But today two fishermen passed by. I heard one of them suggest that since there are so many fish in this pond they should try to catch them all. If that is what they intend to do, I will starve to death," complained the heron.

The crab told this bad news to the fish. They quickly came to the heron, saying, "Because you are wise and experienced, we would like your opinion on this matter."

"We cannot fight against the fishermen," the heron answered. "There is another pond close by. Its water is so clear that you can see the sand at the bottom. If you go there you will be safe."

The fish all liked the idea, but there was a problem. "Without your help it will be impossible for us to get there," they said.

"I would like to help you," responded the heron, "but it would take time, and the fishermen might come any day."

Whoever trusts his enemy deserves whatever punishment he receives.

The fish cried and begged so piteously that at last the heron agreed to take several fish to the other pond each day. But instead of taking the fish to the other pond, the heron took them away and ate them. In the meantime, the other fish kept begging to be taken as soon as possible. Seeing how stupid they were, the heron thought to himself, "This is just the punishment that one who trusts his enemy deserves!"

As the days passed, the crab also wanted to be taken to the other pond. The heron took the crab on his back and flew toward the area where he had eaten the fish. As they approached, the crab saw all the fish bones scattered around and at once understood what had happened. He quickly realized that his enemy was going to kill him, too. Although he was very frightened, he felt that if he didn't try to save himself he would be helping the heron murder him. So he grabbed the heron's neck with his claws, and squeezed so hard that the heron fainted, fell down, and died.

Then the crab went back and told the fish what had happened. Naturally the fish were very upset, but they were glad the heron had been killed, and marked his death as the beginning of a new life for themselves.

"I gave you this example," said the jackal, "so that you can see there are many people who have brought about their own death by not being clever enough. I will tell you a way which will guarantee your own safety as well as bring about the death of the snake."

"I will do as you advise me," the raven assured the jackal.

The jackal outlined his plan: "You should fly very low and look around near the houses for a piece of jewelry.

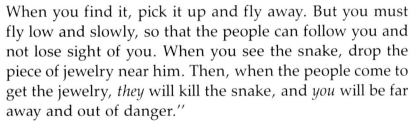

When you find it, pick it up and fly away. But you must fly low and slowly, so that the people can follow you and not lose sight of you. When you see the snake, drop the piece of jewelry near him. Then, when the people come to get the jewelry, *they* will kill the snake, and *you* will be far away and out of danger."

So the raven flew to a nearby house. She saw a woman who had taken off her rings in order to pray. The raven swooped down, grabbed one of her rings, and flew away just as the jackal had told her to do. She dropped the ring close to the snake, and indeed, the people who had followed her killed the snake.

"I told you this story," Dimnah continued, "to make you understand that some things are possible by using your wits that might be impossible if you just used your strength."

Kalilah answered, "But the bull, who has both strength and wisdom, will not be easily defeated."

Dimnah had to agree: "You are right, but do not forget, he still trusts me. I know how to defeat him, just like the hare who killed a lion by using his wits."

"How did he do it?" Kalilah asked.

The Lion and The Hare

*D*imnah said: Many wild animals were living comfortably in a beautiful pasture. But their lives were disturbed by a ferocious lion who lived nearby. One day they all went to the lion to complain: "Each day you go through a great deal of trouble to hunt down one of us for your dinner. Because of you, we always live in fear. We have thought of a way that will keep you happy and will bring us some safety and comfort. If you promise not to attack us, we will send you an animal every day for your meals." The lion agreed.

Time passed, until one day it was the hare's turn to become the lion's dinner. Not wanting to be eaten, the hare said to the other animals: "If you give me a little time, instead of sending me to the lion right away, I will rescue all of you from this tyrant." The animals agreed. The hare waited until it was well past the lion's dinnertime. Then he approached the lion cautiously. The lion was hungry and very angry. When he saw the hare he shouted, "Where is my dinner and why is it so late?" The hare said, "I was bringing you a rabbit, but on the way another lion snatched it. I warned him that it was the king's dinner, but he didn't care. He said, 'This pasture and all the animals in it belong to me, because I am more powerful than the king.' I rushed here to bring you this news!"

The angry lion immediately demanded, "Show me this other lion!" So the hare led him to a deep well with water so clear it reflected an image like a mirror. Then he said, "The lion is in this well. I am afraid of him, but if you hold me up I will show him to you." The lion held the hare,

30

and both of them looked into the well. The lion saw the reflection of himself holding the hare, but thought he was seeing the other lion and the rabbit he had snatched. So he put the hare down and jumped into the well in order to fight the other lion, and he drowned. The hare returned safely, and all the animals were both happy and relieved at the news of the lion's death.

Kalilah considered this tale for a while and then said, "If you can kill the bull without making the lion suffer, it would be much better. You should not bring sadness to the lion, because no wise man who cares about his own safety would cause suffering to his master."

This was the end of their conversation, and Dimnah went to see the lion in order to put his plan into action.

III
THE JACKAL'S SUCCESS

One day when the lion was alone, Dimnah, pretending to be very sad, went to visit him. The lion, surprised to see Dimnah after such a long time, said: "How are you? What brings you here? Did anything important happen?"

Dimnah answered: "Yes, but I have to tell you in private."

"Tell me now," coaxed the lion, "because important matters cannot wait."

So Dimnah began: "It takes courage to say unpleasant things unless one trusts the judgment of the listener. It should be clear to my lord that my words are spoken out of affection and they are not based on suspicion or bad feelings. But, devoted as I am to my lord, I have no choice but to express what seems to be right, because if one does not say the right thing to the king, or conceals his own illness from the physician, he betrays himself!"

The lion interrupted Dimnah, saying: "I believe you are trustworthy enough. Tell me the news. I will think of it as an act of friendship on your part."

So Dimnah explained: "Shanzibah has had many secret meetings with the leaders of the troops and has told them that he has tested and measured your strength and examined your wisdom, and has found weaknesses in both. My lord respected Shanzibah and gave him so much power in all matters that the evil of conspiracy developed in him. It is said, 'When a king realizes that one of his servants has reached the same level as himself, and does not get rid of him, the king brings about his own downfall.'

"You should take immediate action before it is too late and things get out of control. It is said that there are two kinds of people: practical and impractical. The practical people are also of two groups: first there are those who have information in advance and are, therefore, able to plan for whatever happens. The second group are the people who are not frightened or confused by anything and are always able to think of a way out. The impractical people are the ones who are always unsure of what to do and confused by everything that happens and cannot deal with it properly. The story of the three fish," said Dimnah, "is an example of such people."

"What is the story?" asked the lion.

There are always some who can find a way out of a bad situation.

The Fish and The Fishermen

Dimnah explained: Once there were three fish, two practical and one impractical, living in a river basin. It so happened that one day two fishermen passed and decided to bring a net to catch them all. The fish who was wise and practical set to work immediately and escaped from the side where the water passed through. The fishermen returned and blocked two sides of the basin. The other capable fish, who was also wise, said to himself, "This situation is the result of my not paying enough attention to what is going on around me. Now it is time to use my head." Pretending to be dead, the fish floated free on top of the water. One of the fishermen picked the fish up but, thinking it was dead, he threw it back in the water. The fish eventually found a way out and escaped safely. The third one, the confused, impractical fish, was so mixed up he swam up and down like crazy until he was captured.

"I told this story," said Dimnah, "to show my lord that he must punish Shanzibah quickly. A triumphant king eliminates his enemies when he has the opportunity."

The lion looked thoughtful. "Everything you say makes sense," he replied, "but I have been so good to Shanzibah, I can't believe that he has betrayed me."

"That is right," said Dimnah, continuing, "my lord's generosity to the bull made him lose his mind. An ill-natured person is nice until he gets what he wants, and then he wants even more. He plots to obtain even higher positions. The service of a bad person depends on his hopes and fears. When he becomes rich and comfortable he nonetheless clouds the water of kindness and fans the fire of malice. Wise men have said, 'A king must not be unkind to his servants, because they will become hopeless and go over to the king's enemies, yet he must not give them so much wealth that they become daring and interfere in the king's business.' The king must know that honesty cannot be expected from an ill-natured man, just as the sting of a scorpion cannot be controlled even if its tail is tied up for a long time. As soon as it is unfastened it stings, and there is no remedy. And the one who does not listen to the advice of his friends will regret it, just like a sick person who does not follow the advice of his doctor. Thus, I must advise my lord that he who makes his bed of fire and uses a snake as a cushion will not enjoy a tranquil sleep. As soon as an enemy is seen, he should be destroyed before he can do harm."

The lion answered: "You put forth your ideas very strongly, Dimnah. It is clear that if Shanzibah becomes an enemy there is much that he could do against me. As for me, if I had wished it, he could have become my dinner. As you know, his food is grass, mine is meat. But instead I

have given him refuge and a friendship has developed between us. Many times in front of people I have complimented his honesty and trust. Now, Dimnah, if I say the opposite, people will think I am weak and no one will value my promises."

Dimnah answered: "My lord should not content himself by saying 'he could have become my dinner.' He may still not be strong enough to fight against you, but he can gather other people to his side. I am afraid that many of the wild animals may be on his side already, since he has won favor with them."

When at last Dimnah's arguments convinced the lion, he asked, "What must be done?"

Dimnah replied, "When a cavity damages a tooth the only cure is to pull it out. When food is not digested it must be thrown up, and when the enemy cannot be won over by kindness he must be gotten rid of."

The lion said: "I am disgusted with the bull. I will send someone to explain everything to him and let him know that he has my permission to move wherever he wants to go."

Dimnah, fearing that if the bull knew what had been said against him he would be able to prove his honesty and expose Dimnah's lies, quickly said: "That is not a good idea. As long as nothing is said, there are different ways to deal with Shanzibah, but once he knows we distrust him, any act against him becomes difficult, if not impossible. Each word that jumps out of the prison of mouth will be as difficult to bring back as each arrow that is released from a bow. Silence is an invaluable jewel for a king. If Shanzibah learns he is accused, he will deny the charges or prepare for war."

"However," the lion answered, "to destroy one's own friend because of a doubtful rumor is to bring about one's own suffering. A king must reflect on his own deeds as well as the matters of state."

Dimnah bowed his head: "I will obey my lord's command. But my lord must be prepared so that when the bull comes to attack, the traitor does not find him weak. If my lord looks carefully at the bull, he will see his evil nature reflected on his ugly face. His nervousness will be a sign of his hostility. He will anxiously look to the right and left, back and forth, as if he is already in a fight."

The lion nodded in agreement, saying: "This is a good

way to test Shanzibah. If I see such signs I will be sure of his guilt."

When Dimnah saw how angry the lion had become at the bull, he decided to see Shanzibah in order to make him hate the lion, too. But he thought it best to visit the bull by order of the lion himself. So Dimnah asked the lion whether he could visit Shanzibah in order to see what he was up to. The lion nodded.

Dimnah, pretending to be very sad, went to visit Shanzibah. When Shanzibah saw Dimnah's sad face, he said: "I have not seen you for many days. Have you been well?"

Dimnah answered: "How could someone who is at the mercy of someone else's power be well? I am always fearful and trembling! I cannot even take a breath without fear."

The bull seemed surprised. "Why do you feel so hopeless?" he asked.

"Fate," answered Dimnah. "Who can fight against what is ordained by heaven? Who can hold a high position without becoming reckless? Who does not regret his relations with traitors? Who involves himself with a king's business and comes out safely? It is as impossible as going among women and not being charmed by them."

"It seems, from what you have said, that you must be afraid of the lion," observed Shanzibah.

Dimnah answered: "Yes, but it is not fear for myself. You know how much I care about you! You and I have been friends from the time that the lion first sent me to you. I do not see any other choice but to tell you the truth."

"Tell me, old friend, no matter what has happened," coaxed Shanzibah.

Dimnah began: "I heard that the lion said, 'Shanzibah has become too fat. I don't need him and I don't have any fun with him. I will give a party to serve his meat to my friends.' When I heard this I rushed to tell you so that I could prove my friendship and carry out what religion, friendship, and manliness make my duty. And now it is important that you think of a way out."

When Shanzibah heard what Dimnah said he seemed puzzled. "The lion cannot think badly of me, because I have not done anything wrong. Perhaps some people have talked to him behind my back and turned him against me. There are many mean people who serve him, all of them very cunning. The lion has tested all of them time and again, and maybe he thinks that I am like them too. What bad people say and do may cause him to doubt the good ones as well. But to doubt all people because of the evildoing of some is wrong and can have disadvantages, as it had for a duck."

"How?" asked Dimnah.

The Duck and The Star

Shanzibah explained: It is said that a duck saw the reflection of a star in the water. He thought it was a fish and tried many times to catch it. Of course he always failed, and finally he gave up. Then when he saw a real

fish he thought it was only a reflection and did not try to catch it, and so he was always hungry.

"If the lion has believed what mean people have told him about me, it must be because so many others have betrayed him. I do not know of anything I did that might have upset the lion, though it is impossible for two people to be always together, day and night, share each other's sadness and happiness, and never make a mistake. Nobody can avoid mistakes. But I truly think the only mistake I might have made is that sometimes, for his own good, I have disobeyed the lion. Maybe he has taken that as an insult. But surely, in front of other people I have always talked well of him. It might even be possible that the problems of his reign and the responsibilities of the kingdom have caused him to think this way. A king is often satisfied with a traitor and angry with a trusted adviser! Wise men say, 'It is dangerous to jump into the sea with your hands and feet tied, or to kiss a snake's mouth when you are drunk. But it is even more dangerous to serve a king.' "

Shanzibah continued: "It is even possible that my very best characteristics have brought about this split between us. Why, a horse's speed is always the cause of its suffering, and a fruitful tree, because of the heaviness of its fruits, has broken branches, and the beauty of a peacock's tail causes people to pluck its feathers. Besides, goodness amazes those who are not good. A miser is always upset by meeting a generous person, just as a fool is disturbed by a wise man. People without talent refuse to recognize the talent of artists. And sometimes even fate helps the bad people."

When the bull had finally finished speaking, Dimnah observed: "The lion's ideas about you are not caused by the things that you mentioned. They are caused by his own disloyalty and ill nature. The sweet beginning of his friendship has changed into the bitterness of death at the end."

Now Shanzibah became anxious and upset: "I have tasted the sweet, and now it is the time for the pain of the sting! Indeed fate brought me here. What business did I _____ to think of that. I _____ omes so fond of it _____, the petals of the _____ the bee to death. _____ reciate you is like _____ land."

_____ yourself," Dimnah

_____ 'What can I do? I _____ nly good things for _____ trying to get rid of _____ imple task. When _____ they soon succeed, _____ who tried to kill a camel."

"How?" asked Dimnah.

I think that he has got very mad, How Dimnah wanted him two. What did he mean by putting a bee to death.

The Camel and The Lion

Shanzibah explained: It is said that a wolf, a raven, and a jackal who were servants to a lion lived near a public road. A camel who had lost his master came to graze in the nearby pasture. By accident he met the lion, and did not have anything to give him as a gift except his own courtesy and goodwill. The lion spoke softly to him and asked

him whether he wanted to stay in that pasture. The camel answered: "I will do whatever my lord orders me to." So the lion said: "If you like, you can stay here safely and enjoy yourself." The camel happily decided to stay.

Time passed. One day while the lion was hunting for food, he came face to face with a wild elephant. They fought a terrible fight. The lion came back groaning and wounded. He could not hunt for days, and the wolf, raven, and jackal, who depended on the lion for their food, became very hungry. The lion asked them to look around and try to find something for him to hunt so that he could feed them all.

They talked among themselves and said: "What good is the camel to us? He is not our friend, and he is of no benefit to the king. We must convince the lion to kill the camel for food. Remember, whatever is left over will be for us."

"But the lion has protected the camel," the jackal said. "They are friends, and whoever encourages the king to act badly will bring about his own downfall."

But the raven answered, "Don't worry about that. We can always get on the good side of the lion. You stay here till I come back."

The raven went back to the lion. When he asked if they had found anything for him to hunt, the raven answered: "Because we are so hungry, our eyes have become so weak that it is difficult to see, but there is another solution. If the king agrees, all of us will benefit from it."

The lion excitedly demanded that the raven explain what he was thinking of.

The raven said: "The camel is a foreigner among us and he is of no good to the king."

At this, the lion interrupted the raven angrily, saying: "Your idea is dishonorable and unmanly. It is not generous. I have given the camel a home. How could I be cruel to him?"

The raven answered: "I understand that perfectly. However, according to the sayings of the learned men, one person must be sacrificed for the sake of a family, and a family for the sake of a tribe, and a tribe for the sake of a town, and a town for the sake of the king if there is a danger. Surely a way could be found so that my lord will not be accused of unfaithfulness."

The lion began to think.

The raven went back to his friends and said: "The lion

The lies of bad people often succeed.

was angry at first but then he was won over. Now we have to go to the camel and explain to him how unhappy the lion is. We will say, 'We have been happy under the rule of the lion. Now that he is suffering, if we do not offer ourselves as a sacrifice for his food, we will be accused of ingratitude. The best way is for all of us to go to him and thank him for his protection and make it clear to him that we feel we must help him by offering our lives. Each of us will say, 'Today I must be the meal of my lord,' while the rest of us will make excuses and reject the idea. In this way we will be in no danger and we will have expressed our gratitude to the lion.''

They told all of this to the long-necked camel and deceived the poor animal. Then they all went to the lion. After praising the lion, the raven said: ''Our comfort depends on the well-being of our lord. Today I am ready to be sacrificed so my meat can be used for my lord's meal.'' But the others objected, saying: ''Your meat is not enough for the king. You are too small.'' Next the jackal volunteered. Again the others objected. They said: ''Your meat has a bad smell. It does not suit the king.'' Next the wolf offered his own meat. But again they said: ''Your meat causes sickness, it is a deadly poison.'' But when the camel offered himself, everybody said: ''You are right. You should sacrifice yourself because of your friendship.'' Then all the others attacked the camel and tore him apart.

''I told you this story,'' said Shanzibah, ''to teach you that the lies of bad people, particularly when they join together with one another, often succeed.''

Dimnah asked: ''But how then are you going to deal with this problem?''

''There is no other choice except fighting,'' answered Shanzibah.

Dimnah had a ready answer: "A wise man does not rush into danger. Wise men show kindness to their enemy, for it is better to soothe anger by kindness. And you must not underestimate the strength of your enemy, because even if he were weak, he might conquer by lying. Besides, the strength and recklessness of the lion are well known. Whoever underestimates the enemy will regret it, like the sea which underestimated the power of the sea-bird."

"What do you mean?" asked Shanzibah.

The Seabirds

Dimnah began: It is said that a pair of seabirds lived on the shore. When the time for laying eggs came, the female told the male: "We must find a good place for our eggs." The male answered: "But this is a beautiful place—why should we go anywhere else?" The female said: "Why, suppose one day the sea becomes stormy and takes away our children. What could we do?" The male said: "I doubt that the sea is brave enough to do such things to me, and if it does I know how to fight back." But the female was not convinced. She said: "One has to know his own self. What strength do you have that makes you think you can threaten the sea? Forget this silly idea and find a safe place for the eggs. Let me remind you that whoever does not listen to the words of an adviser may end up like the turtle."

"How?" asked the male.

The Ducks and The Turtle

The female explained: It is said that two ducks and a turtle were living in a pond and in time friendship had developed between them. All of a sudden, the water level in the pond began to fall, and the ducks decided to leave. They went to the turtle, saying: "We have come to say good-bye." The turtle became so sad that he started to cry. "Oh, brothers. I, too, can't live without water. Since we

are friends, you must think of a way of taking me with you."

The ducks wanted to help him. They said: "We will miss you so much that wherever we go we won't be able to enjoy ourselves. But if we take you with us you must promise not to open your mouth to answer the calls of the people who will see us on the way."

"I agree," said the turtle. The ducks brought a stick, and the turtle grabbed its middle in his mouth while the ducks took each end and flew away. People, surprised, cried out, "The ducks are taking the turtle away!" The turtle, who had controlled himself at first, could not stand it anymore, and finally opened his mouth to say "It is none of your business!" and fell down. The ducks shouted as they flew by, "You should have taken our advice."

Never underestimate the power of an enemy.

The male seabird said: "I understand the meaning of your story. But let us remain here anyhow." The female laid eggs, and afterward the sea, who had become angry after hearing the birds' conversation, brought his waves to swallow up the birds' babies. The female became very upset and told her husband, "I knew that you could not do anything to the sea, and because of your arrogance we lost our children." The male was equally upset. "Please give me a chance," he begged. "I will do as I have promised and get the children back."

The male seabird went to see the leaders of the other birds and told them: "If you do not work with me the sea will become even more bold, and then all of you will be in danger."

So all the birds went to see the Simorgh, the king of the birds, and explained to him what had happened, adding that if he did not fight back and protect them he could not claim to be the king of the birds anymore. The Simorgh agreed, and encouraged the birds to take revenge. The sea, who was aware of the power of the Simorgh, returned the children of the seabirds.

"I told you this story," said Dimnah, "to show you that you must not underestimate the power of your enemy."

Shanzibah answered: "I am not going to start the fight, but I must protect myself."

Dimnah said: "When you go to the lion, you can tell if he is ready to fight if he is sitting straight and smacking his tail on the ground."

"If such signs are seen," observed Shanzibah, "there will be no doubt about his evil intention."

IV
THE CONSEQUENCES
OF EVIL

Dimnah was so happy with the way his plan was proceeding, he went immediately to see Kalilah.

"What have you done?" asked Kalilah.

Dimnah explained that the lion and Shanzibah would fight soon, and asked Kalilah to go with him to see the lion.

The jackals and Shanzibah arrived at the same time. When the lion saw Shanzibah, he sat straight and moved his tail like a snake. Shanzibah·thought that the lion wanted to attack him. The lion, thinking that Shanzibah also was preparing for a fight, suddenly attacked the bull. They fought fiercely, and both, wounded, bled badly.

Watching the scene, Kalilah felt very badly about the

whole thing. He whispered to Dimnah: "Wait until you see the terrible consequences of your lies."

"What terrible consequences?" asked Dimnah.

Kalilah continued: "The lion's suffering, the fact that he will be accused of betraying his own promises, the waste-

ful shedding of Shanzibah's blood, and your inability to prove your innocence in all this. Let me tell you that the most foolish man is the one who needlessly brings suffering to his master. Wise men avoid war. The adviser who encourages his king to go to war in matters that easily could be solved peacefully proves his own foolishness. Good judgment is more important than a sword, because where there is no good judgment, courage and bravery are of no use.

Your foolishness and arrogance were always clear to me, but I waited to see if you would come to your senses. I have lost my patience. I will tell you how stupid you are and show you the errors of your judgment and evil actions. It is said, 'There is no good in a promise that is not kept, a beautiful sight that people do not know about, wealth that is not spent wisely, unfaithful friendship, and knowledge that is not for the benefit of the people.' When a king has a bad counselor, even if he himself is just, his subjects do not benefit. Intelligent servants are the jewels of a king, but you were so selfish you didn't want anybody else to serve the lion, so that he would put all his trust in you. It is foolish to benefit from someone else's injury, and to expect to have devoted friends without being faithful to them. But nothing will change as a result of this talk, because I can see it is not going to have any effect on you. Advising you is like the man who advised a bird not to try to teach those who are unable to learn.

"What do you mean?" asked Dimnah.

The Monkeys and The Bird

Kalilah explained: It is said that a group of monkeys were living on a mountain. One night the north wind started to blow so harshly that the monkeys began to shiver from the cold. They were looking for someplace to keep warm when suddenly they came across a glowworm. Thinking that it was fire, they put logs on it and blew on it. A bird in a tree nearby saw what they were doing and shouted, "That is not fire." But the monkeys did not pay attention. A man passed by. He said to the bird: "Do not go to so much trouble to advise them. They are not going to listen to you, and you will suffer. Trying to teach such people is like testing a sword on a piece of stone, or concealing sugar under water." But the bird did not pay attention to what the man said, and he flew down to make it clear to the monkeys that the glowworm was not a fire. The monkeys killed him for his trouble.

"You never listen to advice," Kalilah scolded, "but you are going to regret your lies when it is too late, and you will bite your hand and beat your chest, like the clever partner of a foolish man."

"Tell me their story," asked Dimnah.

Two Men and a Bag of Gold

Kalilah began: There were two men, one clever and the other foolish, who happened to be partners in business. They found a bag of gold and wanted to divide it. But the clever man said: "Why should we divide it? It is better to take as much as we need now and hide the rest. We will return to take some whenever we need it." They agreed. So they took some of the gold and buried the rest under a tree nearby. But a day later, the clever man returned and stole the gold.

After a while the foolish man needed gold. So he went to his partner and said: "Let's go and take some of the gold." Together they went to the tree, but of course the gold was not there. The clever man, pretending to be angry, accused the foolish one of stealing the gold. The more the poor fool tried to defend himself, the less he succeeded, and eventually the wise man took him to a judge and explained what had happened.

The judge asked the clever man whether he had any witness or evidence that would prove his partner was a thief. The clever man said: "The tree itself told me that he had stolen the gold." The man's statement so surprised the judge that he decided to hear the tree's testimony himself before pronouncing his verdict.

The clever man went home to his father and said: "You must help me keep the gold. I made up a story about the tree's testimony because I believed I could count on you. If you help me, we will be able to keep the gold that we already have, and might even get another bag."

"What should I do?" asked his father.

The clever man said: "The tree is hollow, so if two people hid in it nobody would see them. You go and stay in the tree tonight, and tomorrow when the judge comes, testify the way you should."

The old man tried to warn his son that lying might bring suffering upon him, and he emphasized: "I hope your lie will not be like the trick of the frog."

"How?" his son asked.

Tricks and lies often
bring about the death of
the liar.

The Frog and The Snake

The father said: A frog was living in a snake's neighborhood. Whenever the frog had children the snake ate them. The frog happened to be friends with a crab. So he went to the crab and said: "Oh, brother, give me some advice. I have a powerful enemy. I can neither resist him nor move anywhere else, since this place is nice and clean." The crab said: "You cannot defeat a powerful enemy except by a trick. A weasel is living nearby. Catch some fish and make a trail of them from the weasel's hole to the home of the snake. When the weasel eats the fish one by one he will reach the snake, and kill him."

And so, by such a trick the frog got rid of the snake. But after a few days the weasel took the same path again, looking for fish. There were none. So when the weasel reached the frog and his children, he ate them all.

"I told you this story," said the father, "so that you know that often tricks and lies bring about the death of the liar."

But the son answered: "Stop this nonsense, Father. This is an easy trick that will make us a big profit."

The greed for money was too great to resist, so the old man agreed to the plan.

The next day the judge went to the tree, and a crowd of people witnessed the scene. The judge asked the tree about the gold. A voice came out insisting that the foolish man had taken it. Naturally, the judge realized that there was someone in the tree. He ordered lots of logs to be brought and put around the tree, and a fire made. The old man waited for a while, until his life was in danger, and then he cried out, begging for mercy. The judge ordered him to be brought out and spoke kindly to him. The old man explained the whole story to the judge and testified to the honesty of the foolish man and the lie of his own son. Then he died of burns from the fire. After receiving his punishment the son headed toward home carrying the dead body of his father. The foolish man, because he was honest, received the gold.

Kalilah continued, saying: "Dimnah, your wisdom and goodness are in such short supply that words cannot express it. And the result of your lies is all around you. You cannot escape its consequences. I always have been afraid to be with you because I remembered what the learned men had said: 'One must avoid bad people even if they are friendly. Friendliness with a bad person is like training a snake. Although the snake charmer goes to great trouble in order to take care of the snake, one day the snake bites him.'

"And you are one of those," continued Kalilah, "with such an ill nature that one must escape as far as possible. How could anyone trust you after you behaved so badly to the lion, who was so good to you? The relationship between you and your friends is like the relationship between the merchant and his friend who stole his merchandise."

"What story is that?" asked Dimnah.

Two Merchants and a Little Boy

Kalilah explained: It is said that a poor merchant whose merchandise consisted of only three hundred kilos of iron decided to go on a trip. He left the iron with a friend. But while the merchant was gone, his friend sold the iron and spent the money. When the merchant returned for his goods, his friend said: "I left the iron at a corner of the house, but a mouse ate it all." The merchant, without showing any surprise, observed: "Yes, mice love iron, and their teeth are sharp enough to chew it well."

Thinking that the merchant believed what he had said, the friend was very happy. But when he left his friend's house, the merchant took his little boy with him. When the friend realized that his little boy was gone, he asked the merchant if he had seen him.

The merchant reported: "I saw an eagle carrying a boy."

"But that is impossible," cried out the friend. "How could an eagle pick up a boy?"

The merchant laughed, saying: "In a town where a mouse can eat three hundred kilos of iron, an eagle must be able to pick up a little boy." The friend understood what had happened. So he told the merchant the truth about his iron and asked him to return the boy.

"I told you this story," continued Kalilah, "to help you understand that because of what you have done to the lion nobody will trust you anymore."

The conversation between Kalilah and Dimnah had reached this point when the lion stopped fighting with Shanzibah.

When a king has a bad counselor, his subjects will suffer.

V

THE TRUTH COMES OUT

When the lion saw Shanzibah fallen and bleeding to death, his anger cooled down. He thought for a while and said to himself: "What a pity to see Shanzibah so wounded. He had such wisdom and intelligence. I am not sure whether I was right in what I have done. Is it possible that in reporting to me about Shanzibah, Dimnah has betrayed me?"

When these sad thoughts appeared on the lion's face, Dimnah stopped talking to Kalilah and went over to the lion. "Is there anything the matter?" he asked. "There is no better time than this moment for celebration, since the king is triumphant and the enemy is defeated."

The lion answered thoughtfully: "Whenever I remember Shanzibah's hard work, and knowledge, I am sure I will be sad. I must admit that he was the nicest person among my subjects."

Dimnah said: "That animal did not deserve any mercy. This victory will always be remembered as a historic event. For the enemy of the king there is no prison except the grave and no punishment except a sword. The wise ruler must stay close to learned and honest people even if he does not like them, and he must keep away crafty ones even if they appeal to him."

The lion felt a little better, but he felt bad because of the hasty manner in which he had killed the bull.

One night on his way home, after being up late with the lion listening to him talk about Shanzibah and how he missed him, the leopard was going home when he happened to pass the home of Kalilah and Dimnah. Kalilah was talking to Dimnah, reminding him of what he had done. The leopard stopped and listened.

Kalilah said: "You have done a terrible thing and betrayed the king. But you cannot escape the consequences of your lies and you will soon be punished. I am sure that none of the animals will excuse you. Everybody will ask for your execution. I do not want to be with you anymore."

Dimnah answered: "Put this nonsense out of your mind and be happy that the enemy is dead. Though I must admit that at the time that I decided to cause Shanzibah's death, I didn't realize what a vicious thing I was doing. I was carried away by greed and envy."

When the leopard heard this conversation he went to see the lion's mother and made her promise not to disclose to anyone what he had to say. The next day the lion's mother went to see her son. She found him very sad. The lion explained: "I know I have killed Shanzibah, yet I can't help but remember his goodwill and service. Although I try hard to forget him, it is impossible, and whenever I think about governing correctly, I realize I won't be able to find anyone who will advise me so well."

His mother said: "What you say proves Shanzibah's innocence. If you had thought about the report that you received concerning Shanzibah's treason and overcome your anger, the truth would eventually have come into the open."

The lion acknowledged: "I have been thinking a lot about Shanzibah in order to find some way to excuse myself for having killed him. But the more I think, the more I am sorry for it. Poor Shanzibah was not without sound judgment and a good nature. The accusations of envious people are always based on such things. I did not neglect him, so he had no reason to become my enemy. Although it is too late now, I would like to do an investigation and find out the truth. If you know or have heard anything about this situation, please let me know."

His mother answered: "Yes, I have heard something, but I cannot tell it to you now. Wise men have pointed out the disadvantages of disclosing secrets."

The lion shook his head angrily. "The learned men say many different things, and intelligent people decide what is necessary at the moment. Remember, to conceal the secrets of criminals is like sharing their crimes."

"What the wise men say about forgiveness and kindness is well known," the lion's mother advised her son, "but these sayings concern crimes that do not harm society. Whenever there is a crime that harms the public, the king is responsible. Therefore, there cannot be any forgiveness. It was Dimnah, the jackal, who encouraged you to kill Shanzibah, and he is wicked."

The lion reflected on the matter for a while and then decided to take action. He summoned his troops, and sent for his mother as well. Then he asked for Dimnah. When Dimnah arrived he asked the reason for the gathering. The lion's mother told him: "The king is deciding your punishment. Since your betrayal has come into the open, and your lies about his dear and honest friend have been discovered, he must not allow you to live."

But Dimnah did not seem upset. He replied calmly:

"Our ancestors have revealed to us that the better a man is, the more trouble he has. And the more he serves a king honestly, the more he endangers himself. That is because both the friends and enemies of the king are against him, friends because they are envious, and enemies because they do not want anybody to help the king. That is why some people prefer loneliness to being with other people. They prefer God almighty to his creatures, since God would not reward goodness with evil and there will never be any injustice in his acts.

"But," said Dimnah, "people's actions are not just. Sometimes they grant criminals the same reward as honest people, and other times they punish their honest advisers as if they were criminals. They act according to their feelings. Good and bad are the same in their view.

"A successful king," Dimnah went on to say, "is the one who prefers righteousness, and the best characteristic of a king is his love for honest servants. The king knows, and the people here can testify to the fact, that there were no bad feelings between the bull and me which could have made us enemies. I advised my lord according to what I believed was my duty. Then my lord acted the way he felt was suitable. I never thought the reward for my service would be my lord's wanting my life."

When the lion heard Dimnah's plea, he said: "The judges must investigate Dimnah's deed. It is not just to pronounce a verdict without first examining the evidence."

Dimnah then said: "Which judge could be more correct and just than my lord? If a thorough investigation is to be done, I am sure that I will prove worthy of the king's trust. If I had committed this crime I would not have begged you for this investigation. I hope that my lord will appoint a

To let bad people live is as bad as to kill good people.

judge who does not resent me, and make sure that any evidence be reported to him daily so that the king himself can examine it."

One of the attendants cried out: "Dimnah's words are not spoken to honor the king but to save his own life."

Dimnah answered: "If I do not attempt to protect myself when I am in danger, how can anybody else have hope for me? What you said only shows your own foolishness."

But the lion's mother interrupted him: "You surely have amazed me by your speech."

Dimnah said: "Indeed this is the place for speeches, since it will be heard by wisdom's ear."

The lion's mother, unable to contain herself any longer, then shouted: "Oh, you traitor! You still think you will be rescued by lies or magic?"

Dimnah answered: "My lord knows that no traitor has the courage to speak out in front of him. I am not saying these words because I fear death. Although I do not wish for it, I know there is no escape from it. But even if I had thousands of lives, if I knew giving them up would help my lord, I would give them all in an hour. But that is not the situation. My lord should consider the consequences of his acts. He should not waste good servants because of envious people."

When the lion's mother realized that Dimnah's lies and honeyed words seemed to be convincing her son, she told the lion: "Your silence is proof of what Dimnah says, you have already destroyed your best advisers," and she left angrily. The lion ordered Dimnah to be imprisoned and demanded that the judges start their investigation.

When they took Dimnah to prison and chained him, Kalilah went to see him. When he saw Dimnah chained he could not prevent himself from crying and said to him: "Oh, brother! How it hurts to see you in such trouble! What pleasure can life have for me after this? I predicted all of this and advised you, but you did not pay attention. You have always hated advice. Your pride overcame your wisdom and intelligence. I told you the saying of the wise men, 'Diligent people will die before their natural time of death.' They did not mean death of the body but sorrow and pain which would make life more difficult than death—like the situation that you are in at this moment."

Dimnah answered: "You always told me the right thing and advised me correctly, but greed and ambition weakened my judgment and made your advice useless. I know that I have planted the seeds of this tragedy, and one has to harvest what one plants, though he may regret it afterward. But I am frightened more when I think that because of our long friendship you may be accused too. Do not tell them you knew about my plot. They will believe your testimony."

Kalilah answered: "As the wise men say, no man can stand torture and pain. In order to free himself from punishment, one may say anything, wrong or right. I do not see any way out for you except that you confess to your guilt, so that at least you will be absolved in the other world. Surely you will be executed."

"I will think about it and let you know my decision," said Dimnah.

A wild animal who was Dimnah's cellmate and was resting in a corner heard the conversation between Kalilah and Dimnah but said nothing. Meanwhile, Kalilah returned home. Sad and depressed, he went to bed. He rolled and wallowed until at last he stopped breathing.

The next day the lion's mother told her son: "To let bad people live is as bad as to kill good people. He who keeps an evil person alive shares his evil." Upset, the lion ordered the judges to hurry their investigation and to bring their charges against Dimnah in front of the public.

So the judges called a public meeting. One of them addressed the audience and said: "The king has tried very hard to find out what, if anything, Dimnah has done, because he wants to be sure your verdict is a just one. Therefore, if any of you know anything about Dimnah's guilt, he or she must testify."

When the judge finished speaking everybody was quiet. Nobody said a word. When Dimnah observed the silence, he said: "If I were guilty I would be very happy about your silence. However, I am not guilty, and the one who tells the truth here can save or waste a life. But if anyone is about to speak without evidence or reason and cause my blood to be shed, he should know that what happened to the foolish man might also happen to him."

"What is the story?" the judges asked.

The Old Physician and The Foolish Man

Dimnah explained: Once in one of the cities of Iraq lived an excellent physician. He was well known for his skill in finding remedies for different illnesses and his knowledge of various drugs. But he had become blind in his old age. There was a foolish man who claimed to be a physician, and when he saw the old doctor was about to retire, he tried to make a name for himself.

The governor of the city happened to have a daughter who, while giving birth to a baby, became ill. He took her to the old physician. After examining her carefully, he recommended a drug that had to be made up from several substances. Because of his blindness, the old doctor was not able to make it himself, but the foolish man claimed that he could. Without having any knowledge of drugs, he went to the laboratory, made a poisonous mixture, and gave it to the woman, who immediately died. For revenge, the governor gave a portion of the fatal mixture to the foolish man himself.

"I told you this story to show you that an ignorant act may have a terrifying consequence."

When Dimnah finished, the animals were quiet. The judges ordered that Dimnah be returned to prison. While in prison, Dimnah received the news of Kalilah's death.

The next day the chief justice reported to the lion what had happened. The lion explained everything to his mother. His mother seemed very upset and thought deeply. At last she spoke. "In what I say I may upset the king, but if I avoid saying what is right, I will be guilty of not advising him rightly."

The lion answered: "There must be no fear or caution in giving advice."

His mother then said: "The king cannot distinguish between right and wrong. Dimnah is very evil and sooner or later will find an opportunity for an act so awful that

the king would not be able to imagine it, and then it will be too late to punish him."

Then she got up abruptly and left.

The next day the judges brought out Dimnah and again gathered the people and asked for testimony. Since nobody talked against Dimnah, the chief justice himself spoke to Dimnah: "Although the people are silent, in their hearts they believe you are guilty. What is the pleasure of living in such a situation? It is to your advantage to confess your guilt and by repentance at least be absolved in the other world. You surely know that dying with a good name is far better than living with a bad one."

But Dimnah replied: "The judge must not pronounce a verdict on the basis of his own suspicion or others' without any evidence."

The judges reported all of this to the lion. The lion, in turn, explained all of it to his mother. His mother grew very angry. At last she said: "Long live the king! Dimnah will attempt to use his terrible lies against the king and create treason in the nation. The result of this will be worse than what he did to Shanzibah."

The lion listened to these words thoughtfully and then asked his mother: "Who told you about Dimnah's evil deeds? Tell me so that I will have a proper reason for killing him."

But his mother said: "Unless I have his permission I cannot tell you someone else's secret. Let me ask permission first."

So the lion's mother went to see the leopard and said to him: "The king's generosity and kindness toward you is well known. It is now your duty to repay his kindness by testifying to what you know."

The leopard answered: "If I had thousands of lives, I

would sacrifice all of them for the comfort of my lord."

Then they went to the lion, and the leopard told him about the conversation between Kalilah and Dimnah that he had overheard, and testified to it in front of the other animals. When the leopard's testimony was heard by the wild animal who had overheard Kalilah and Dimnah speaking in prison, he sent someone to say that he would testify too. The lion ordered him to explain what he knew and asked: "Why did you not say this before?" The animal answered: "One witness alone is not enough to prove someone is guilty."

So by these two testimonies Dimnah was convicted. The lion ordered him to be imprisoned, chained, and starved to death.

This, then, is the result of lying and the end of a person who is cruel to others.